I0882929

salmonpoetry

Publishing Irish & International Poetry Since 1981

PRAISE FOR PREVIOUS WORK BY SU LOVE

"Direct, unvarnished, luminous"
SPENCER REECE, *Road to Emmaus*

"Beautifully marries attention and evanescence"
ALISON HAWTHORNE DEMING, *Stairway to Heaven*

"Heartbreaking power of plain language"
ELIZABETH HOOVER, *Minneapolis Star Tribune*

"Su Love writes with eccentric grace and clarity"
DEBORAH KEENAN, *Willow Room, Green Door*

The Memoir of Mona Lisa
and Other Poems

Su Smallen Love

Published in 2019 by
Salmon Poetry
Cliffs of Moher, County Clare, Ireland
Website: www.salmonpoetry.com
Email: info@salmonpoetry.com

Copyright © Su Love, 2019

ISBN 978-1-912561-60-5

All rights reserved. No part of this publication may be reproduced or transmitted in any form or by any means, electronic or mechanical, including photography, recording, or any information storage or retrieval system, without permission in writing from the publisher. The book is sold subject to the condition that it shall not, by way of trade or otherwise, be lent, resold or otherwise circulated without the publisher's prior consent in any form of binding or cover other than that in which it is published and without a similar condition, including this condition, being imposed on the subsequent purchaser.

Cover & Title Page Art: Leonardo da Vinci, *Mona Lisa* (detail)
Cover Design & Typesetting: *Siobhán Hutson*

Printed in Ireland by Sprint Print

Salmon Poetry gratefully acknowledges the support of
The Arts Council / An Chomhairle Ealaíon

Contents

The Memoir of Mona Lisa

The Memoir of Mona Lisa

What did Lazarus gain or lose
When he was raised from his dark room?

I

I opened the door, midday. Why did I open the door?
Restless, lonely, a young bride, I opened the bedroom door.
The room fell into me; I saw my husband, Francesco;
I did not understand at first; reclining on our bed,
Francesco's expression new, rapturous; light and shadow made
Of him a lattice; he was joined with a man, full in the
Man's mouth; both nude, gorgeous, in vestures of pleasure deeply
Themselves, like a painting never seen, breath coming fast for

Both, none for me. I closed the door but could move no more than
The dust motes lit in the slant I slipped from. I did go back
The next day, and the next, but I did not open the door.
Against it I leaned ear and mind. Wedded, I had made my plight.
If I were to give Francesco sons, I needed to know.
I would clothe myself with this surface. I would be a man.

II

I stole clothes from my husband, altered what I could.
I practiced Francesco's gestures, his carriage.
One night I dressed and waited, with one candle lit.
When he opened the bedroom door, an unspoken
Question drew dark across Francesco. Like sampling
Silk, testing its weight and drape, and finding it
Inadequate, poor quality, he pulled the clothes from me
Thudding like a bolt unwinding on the cutting table,

Until his rude hands fell empty.
I stood up in my nakedness, female,
To face him. Air, sharp with points and planes,
Cluttered my lungs. I took asylum
In my virtue. I knew that what of me
Could break had a grain. I yielded.

III

I trained my lungs to hold back my heart,
So I could hear something else than fear.
"I know," I said. "I am not asking
You to give up your lover." He wanted,
He said, a legitimate heir,
Nothing else, otherwise I could do
As I wished. He would let me paint.
I said, "If I were a man, you might—"

(Was I at a threshold or an edge,
I did not know.) For a moment,
Between us was the least of boundaries.
"Tell me," I said. "We will find our way.
What is his name?"
My back was braced with butterflies.

IV

Leonardo of Verrocchio's bottega
Chose him. It was only a rite of passage
At fourteen. Except. Except how beautiful
Leonardo was, tender, and outrageous.
He bought caged songbirds at market, simply to

Set them free. As Francesco spoke, it seemed he
Found in his soul's house a room he had never
Known was there. Leonardo had other boys

But Francesco had solely Leonardo.
He could not let him go. Not even after
Leonardo left Florence—. Francesco quieted,
The points and lines of the air formed pyramids.
He reached for my hair, cupped it, traced my lips, one
Finger slipped into the little hollow there.

V

"Francesco tells me you are a good boy."
Leonardo appeared in the doorway
Of my sitting room the next day. April
Light burned sienna in turns of his curls.
An unsettling heat burned in me. There was
Secrecy but no privacy in my
Husband's house. I had no answer for him
So said nothing. I mixed shades of ochre,

Wanting to capture the moment before.
I was painting a pair of wild horses,
The feeling I had of fear around them.
To my surprise, I did not mind him watching,
As he did, for time suspended. "Francesco,
He finally said, "is a badly broken horse."

VI

Francesco said, "I hear you met
Leonardo. He left today for
Milan." I poured myself into
Francesco's silence. He would say
Nothing more. He entered me and
I filled with loneliness. I sought
Francesco's eyes; he would not look
At me. I touched his face and he

Turned out of my hands. I touched his
Waist – he pinned my arms like folded
Wings. I turned my head to the sky
Through the window. He finished, said,
"Lift your hips to ensure a child."
Then he left the bed and the room.

VII

The morning my son was born, the hot air darkened.
Multitudes of swifts churned as one ominous
Funnel, skirling black. Candles were lit. The midwife
Caught and kept the baby. "Please," I said. Francesco
Strode into the room. "Boy," the midwife said. He took
My baby and left. Dark stars beat me. My body
Fell into a well of separate bodies, bereft
Unbiddable. The swifts wailed and frenzied the hours

Hours til Francesco returned. Where was my baby?
"My son is with his milkmother. My son, not yours.
Understand this, Lisa." The terrible birds gaped.
Breath worked me like a machine, winched me.
On the iron river, rain spilled its metal beads.
(The rain fell without ceasing for eleven months.)

VIII

"I will not sit for him just so you can—"
Francesco's eyes flashed. "He asked to paint you. I agreed.
It is convenient. On commission, Leonardo can
Come and go freely here without question. He will paint you."
I picked up my pestle to crush pigments, to grind down my
Desire to have nothing to do with this into what must
Be endured. I put on the jewels Francesco had given
Me, turned my wedding band, then took it and all the jewels off.

Leonardo said nothing. He took up his brush, forgot
His brush. Shadows declaimed their forms. Sunlight dialed the room.
I pressed the heel of my right hand on the back of my left.
"You wished to paint my portrait, yet you have not moved."
"Francesco told you, did he, that I asked for you? Does he
Tell everything?"
"Close to nothing."
"Where it's most interesting."

IX

Leonardo began to sing,
Not to me but for me. His eyes
Steadied on me, unlike any
Other man, without desire
Or judgment. From out of time
With whatever power pushes
The night, his song-flung vision
Enclosed me in serenity

Vast and lit. He painted a bridge
That crossed to nowhere and a road
That wound unreliably toward
A storm that aroused the air.
"I have kept you," he said, "like a
Market bird. Come, paint next to me."

X

After the year of unending rain, failed crops yielded
Famine, plague, and evangelical fever.
At street corners, wooden boxes appeared, locked, with
Slits to slip in anonymous denunciations of
Adultery or sodomy. Many accused were,
Without investigation, fined, shamed, flogged, maimed,
Imprisoned, and exiled. Francesco's wealth secured
His senate seat and strengthened his general contempt.

Once, Leonardo drew a male nude from the waist
Down and from the waist up, the man split into two
Men, four lungs, two hearts, two minds, their arms twined as
One being. "Pleasure and Pain," he called it. They held
A reed between them. "Reeds in the light show only
A little. The wounds they inflict are poisonous."

XI

Every night I lit candles, kept them burning with
My silhouette in view to the street, to protect
My men from the night patrols, hunting for trouble.
What pulled me from one night to the next was desire
To be held, which merely brittled me. The doors of

My imagination too often opened to
Leonardo's pleasure, Francesco's rapture,
Until the first free skylark relieved my watch.

I don't remember how many nights were like this
Until Francesco reared and threw Leonardo.
"Do not leave me to explain your unfinished work—
I got that commission for you. I." Leonardo
Did abandon much. This time he never returned.
Loneliness fissured everything I painted.

XII

Francesco was imprisoned but politics
Released him. He returned leached. My relief
Changed to alarm. I reached out both hands which
He unmet. The window threw lattice shadows
On him like a scribe cancelling a passage.
His hands fisted. "I am sending you to
A convent, Lisa. You are too much like him—"
His fists emptied their power. I crumpled—

Stars wheeled, beat. I fell against a threshold.
What was custom now? Against caution, I
Found Leonardo. "Please," I said, "Take me
With you." His eyes calculated like a cat,
Point A to point B. He touched my left hand,
Turned it over, cradled it in his palm.

XIII

But, he did not say *andiamo*.
"Lisa, Bella, you must not
Grow lovelier." He queried me
As if I were made of light—How
Can you not love the one with whom
You are beautiful? "We have
Our proof. The portrait has no
Vanishing point." I turned, I left him.

As I approached my house, I saw fire.
Saw Francesco throw my paintings to fire.
The weft of my spine burned, cracked like kindling.
I went back to Leo, who was with two men
Readying four horses that tamped their hooves
Like pestles. He looked up, to me, "Ready?"

XIV

I followed him the rest of his days, not
As woman, nor man, but as painter, that is watcher,
Shadow to his light, light to his shadow.
For a long time, I thought, though I loved, I failed love
And love failed me. I studied the questions of
Form and perspective, surface and relationship
Alert to understand what it was
My heart led me to. It is this place:

I have made a room of myself
For others to leave from
Such that when you turn away
You return confirmed to something
In your life as radiant,
Necessary, and true.

Letter from Spain

Note from the Sea

At the end of a long, restless journey with no clear beginning, I arrived at a window that opened like doors onto the treetop of a palm that rolled the rain like those toys made of ramps and drops for balls to travel and signal some other action, if only our delight. There, finally, I slept, rich with water, my breath cycling. Everything miraculously stayed beyond the window, out with the Spanish sea, even time.

Released, silent, under the plane of foreign tongues, in the language of rain, rain anointing me, adorning me with rings traveling outward on the surface of myself. No one knows where I am or where I have been. No phone, no internet. To all who approached me, I said, "no entiendo" like magic words, and they left me be. Nothing for me to answer, to repair, to take on, to carry.

The rain falls slowly enough to process the tensile perfection of raindrops, globes, worlds falling, respiring into earth and deeper earth, into ocean, lifting into air and deeper air.

No entiendo. Enough, though, for a poem. Every poem is a kind of thank you note: "Here, observing, thank you."

El Masnou, by the Sea

I thought it would be romantic, the sea. It is only the sea. Magnificent without my ideas.

Here, like everywhere, a first bird sings the morning in. A recycling truck pours a crashing of glass. A dog barks. Yarn-bombed trees sport crocheted skirts. The weather is unusual. People work where they can get work. Couples sit without speaking. One who seemed alone stands up to greet another, is blocked by chairs; they hug awkwardly, the chair wants a group hug. The friends slip off their shoes under the table of coffee and beer, their talk falls like rain. Teens in threes take selfies. People walk with their eyes on their phones. Women comb their hair with their fingers. Children step on only the red squares, not the white or gray ones.

A relief to rest, away from the dominant, the dollar, the endgame, the direct, the driver. A relief to rest, away from the necessary articulation toward, if not love (let us lower our standards), then compatibility, reciprocity.

Forty years ago, I first saw this sea when I was sick with food poisoning. I sat on the sand and watched my companions run, receding from me, into joy and surf. I dozed until they returned, wet and gritty, like played-out dogs.

Everything this beach is made of is something broken. What's next, the questions. What was, the memories. Up and forward, down and back. Thoughts, like the black bloated rat or the gray drowned shirt make no net progress, neither toward land nor toward open sea.

In the evenings, cruise ships draw the horizon line. The ships look like layer cakes with lit frosting, slowly turning on a platter. The pool-cleaning robot dances adagio, glissades, pirouettes, all evening, into the next day.

Spain is dry, scrappy, good for vineyards and olive groves. The seawalls are graffiti-tagged and tagged over. You must go inland for green, behind the yard walls, for ivy, palm, hibiscus, rhododendron, for magpies, sparrows with red berets, green South Americans, and doves that sound like dogs with laryngitis barking through mesh screens.

I learned my name means "his" or "her" in Spanish. Who am I to belong to? The dog on the beach waits with the patience of dogs with its toy while its human scrolls the iPhone. There, a couple laughs, holding hands and swinging them in large arcs, like kids do. They might take off.

Madrid

Many statues of angels rise above the city, and one falls. The fallen angel grabs the snake of his groin.

It is a late, late-night city, a slow-starting city. In the early morning, a few people traipse through litter, cigarette butts, pee, past a pair of boots, underwear, and vomit. At a corner, three prostitutes confer, share a light. Tired pretty men in tired pretty clothes walk, maybe home, maybe to work.

At the church of the holy cross, people queue up for an hour or two to touch the statue of Jesus, who stands in a plexiglass closet. There is a small opening to reach through to touch his right foot. A woman used her turn to put her baby's hand through the little doorway. Many people, women and men, reach through and up and stroke Jesus' leg sensually. One man pumped Jesus' toes like he was jerking a cock.

In the museum, after all the crucifixions, beheadings, rapes, and the private thoughts of prostitutes, the abstract art is a relief.

Saturday in Madrid

On Saturday, the streets fill with people; people in the sun of the plaza, people in the shade of the narrow streets, Spanish, French, German, English, as if it were a festival, the festival of Saturday.

The golden light of October slants through the drying trees, and roses still bloom in El Retiro. A man says, “What is fidelity actually? We must live in the present.” The woman next to him drifts away.

Set in a window, a finch in a much-too-small birdcage spends its days trying to jump to a new perch, its body readying and readying, but there is no other perch.

In the park, an unseeable child calls from within the box-hedge maze. A man responds, “Turn right. Turn left.”

Letter from Spain

I did not mail my hand
Reaching through the letterbox
Of Spain. I meant to—
No voice there telling me
Turn left, turn right. Once
That voice was clear, *right, right*—
Not until I turned left
Did I know the voice to be
A host of groaning angels.
Man. One angel then broke
In: *okay, okay, hold on*—
In Madrid, where one angel
Always falls, I was
The unlikely guest of
A church bishop who, over
Juice and cookies, said to pray
Simply ask for what you need,
But—loosely translated—
You must first fold your hands.
The Bishop's bird was wild but
Injured, blinded by a cat.
She will not speak against
Him, so she sings little.
I held on too long, held
Back too much. I need
Platform shoes to see
Above the box hedge.
The Bishop's bird on its perch
Dips, side-steps, and dips
Ready to mail herself—
Not that the bird belongs
To the Bishop, nor
An angel to a boy—

I misplaced the letter from
Spain, the letter that was
My relieved hand lifting
Lines from a sea-rain's score.
I meant to send you
This letter, my hand; this note,
My mind; this book, my body.

Lines That Do Not Exist but We Draw Them

Negative Space

After Benjamin McVey

The towers, he said, when finally he could
Draw them, became the line between.

On the river bridge, people stop for the
Oncoming rush and spray. One watches on
The other side, looking at the line after.

After the bridge fell, the river resumed
Its line, untroubled, even unchanged.

On the river bank, an oak table stands
On fluted legs, chairless, opened for its leaf.

Personal Line

After Barbara Ras

Of course there was death, from early on, the president, my uncle, then butterflies we caught in jars, then Vietnam my whole childhood

of anxiety watching my little brother, the brown-painted door, and the TV, more tear-bombing on campus, police with bats, and the solace when the doorknob finally turned with its pop, the door with its metallic scrape, my parents returned from the U for one revolution

the car's back tire picked up the kitten from the road, carried it like a Ferris wheel, left it looking perfect so that I was not really sure if it happened, what I saw, and I carried the kitten to the grass and sat with it, unmoving

we lined the darkened hallways of school, practiced for when the bombs would drop, sat with our heads down on our knees, our hands on our heads to protect us, of course, we never practiced for what came after

kisses that didn't mean anything except that we had nothing to say, and one girl developed curves early and hung beads to mark her bedroom from the basement where we danced to "Oh Mandy" before she eloped, it was said, and disappeared

like the boys who liked me because they really wanted to know if the Honey Queen who stood in a roomful of bees at the state fair three summers for scholarship money, my best friend, was she seeing anyone, all except that one boy I fell asleep with on the couch after work after school, simply exhausted of course, but who would believe us when we said, after drilling for oil, piping oil, shipping oil, warring for oil, spilling oil, fracking oil, freighting oil, five trains an hour, derailing trains of burning oil, that harvesting solar power was too expensive, some logic missing

written on all the milk cartons but when I found fine locks of hair on the seat of the port-a-potty and a child's shirt down there with the shit, of course the cops said it meant nothing, and yet

this world remained tender with lost mittens fitted on low tree branches and lost dolls set on curbs to give them a better chance of being found, with daisies slipping through cracks in the sidewalks, and small bees landing on open books, pointing precisely to the words *we may breathe*.

Line Out of Line

i.

if I could master the line I could give
you the taste of a thickly buttered
crescent roll dipped in coffeemilk, the weight
of a brush to draw through your mother's hair
a rain puddle reaching up cool under
the bridge of your foot if I could master
the line I give you
my name, my division
but the line wild, the line out of line

ii.

in the tree of words, life
and body have the same mother
                                                            to remain, to persevere, continue
                                                            see leave
                                                            see amount left over after
division to be carried pulled, pushed, the line
breaks soil, draws itself up, out, down
the line tracks you, tracks itself, the pencil on chase
gets to where it is only by the path it takes
                                                            the body moves of its own mind
                                                            the pencil moves of its own mind
            you negotiate the field between
to draw life is to bequeath a track
                                                            show up show up show up
                                                            remain leave leaf love
you can persevere and still lose
            shift and still lose
            love and still lose
that's not the story line
            be the remnant   years later you see what losing won

iii.

the line leans forward leans
back by degrees changed by
fracture released the
through line the line through
you give me ground place
and displace me between
us a fault line either side of
which sutures we pierce
we two remnants we
one yellow dress cut on the bias
two vectors of slip

Some of Us Are Drawn to Those Who Don't Want Us

After Jane Hirshfield

We found the mallard duckling floundering
at the front curb of the Walker Art Center
after somehow making it across the nine-lane
Hennepin-Lyndale bottleneck in rush hour.
We brought the duckling back to Loring Park,
set him in the pond. The duckling zoomed across
the water calling "Mama! Mama!"—
it was unmistakable, his rapture of the spared.
Once at his mother's side,
she grabbed him by the neck,
shoved him under water,
again and again and again
as the duckling struggled against
death, against her whom he loved,
and who knows how or why
but he escaped and swam
back to shore so fast, small wings outstretched
in that kind of pain you have seen.

I whistled to him like I did for my budgies.
In my cupped hands, he warmed.
When we released him in the duckling nursery,
he disappeared, enveloped in a yellow pond
of small salvaged mallards.

To hold a heart—how
Grief, too, becomes
                    many years
                    meaningless
                                        have I been
                                        in that fortunate world

Life Drawing: First Session, Six Poses

(5 minutes)
I'm after a line, and I'm out of words.
There's a naked man, very nice, to pose,
however I want. I have no idea
what I want. Something occurs on the path
from my eyes to the page. The line is not
what I see.

(5 minutes)
Life drawing feels like learning to hold back
the extra limbs of the "E," to tame the curves
of the "S" and lay it down facing the right
direction. It feels like learning to say
what I mean.

(5 minutes)
Something occurs and the line is not right
but I like it anyway. No reason.

(5 minutes)
[ ]

(5 minutes)
The hands and ears
give me trouble so I erase them. That
space, though, between the man's arm and torso,
my line comes close to that. Should I be
concerned that I am more comfortable with
negative space? About that, my painter friend,
untroubled by hands and ears, says only
positive things.

(5 minutes)
I'm still learning to say what I mean. What
I want is the line that draws you to me.

Life Drawing: Second Session

I'm the only one who has come to draw
and the model is Jessie, not Dave.
I envy Jessie's ease with which she
undresses while I busy myself with
the placement of my pencil, paper,
paper, pencil. There is no pencil
sharpener. She takes her first pose. She
looks sad but says she is tired, got in
after two this morning, long drive from
Rhode Island. Plus, it is almost raining.
My line today is darker. I erase
less. I'm trying to be accurate but
also less tight. That's my nemesis,
"try," try to be right, try to be good,
but I hold myself back, hold it in, tight,
uptight, spinster, always holding it,
except when I don't, then it's disaster.
Always. I don't trust myself after—
well I'm here, and I'm drawing, and I'm
so bad, I laugh. I briefly worry
that Jessie thinks I'm laughing at her
but sure she doesn't, she's been doing
this a long time. Still, she sighs a lot.
All down the inner side of her right arm
several bright scratches overlay a
large bruise. My line ignores these, also her
nose and mouth. I look and draw and look and
still the line appears a caricature,
not life. Am I drawing life? If I were,
I would draw the closing of her sad eyes,
her breath, and her swallows.

Life Drawing: Fifth Session

The instructions
are clear enough,
start with the head,
mark the shoulders
and hips on the page,
then fill in the rest.
The rest!
The body proves
strange. The line that
means folds of skin
at the neck, under
breasts, above the
waist looks the same
as the line that means
collar bones diving
to pond the voice.

Life Drawing: Seventh Session, Five Poses

(5 minutes)
I lost my pencil, I'm late, the model
is annoyed, was just about
to leave but here I am.
"I'm an artist," she says.
And I'm not. Cue the old tapes.
An empty space to fill. I draw my lines.

(5 minutes)
The way I draw her, she's Joni Mitchell,
would rather paint than sing. *Blue,*
here is a shell for you.

(5 minutes)
Words flatten into the line
that flattens. Nothing
for the lovely cord
of collarbone.

(10 minutes)
                    This one
          under water
                         she wavers

(20 minutes)
To indicate the long reclining body,
                                                  that hand will have to do, draped
                                                                              over the iliac crest,
index finger touching the thigh socket crease,
                                                            resting in the blue there.

Life Drawing: Diptych with Dead Bird and Poppy

Seated, a stillpoint
in a festival of grass,
an emaciated angel
with pin-feathered wings,
with webbed ribs, femur, tibia,
leans its head in its wing-palm.

The old red poppy, blown out,
can't hold light, can't hold its cup,
sweat shines in its remnant curves.
Red pools dark in its ragged frays.
The secret clock that dialed the bee,
unfurled, a pinwheel paused.

Life Drawing: Nothing Like

Summer clouds with pines and irises in them,
Or yellow peonies, their inner petals casting gold
Shadows on the outer petals, or the river's edge
Where you are closer in size to lichen than to sky, as
Mysteriously placed, or a new poppy dancing like
Isadora Duncan with a handful of light before
Drawing her fingertips together to close the day.

Life Drawing: We Would Be Egrets

Flexing our knees
Would unbuckle
Us from gravity
Into air
Dangle our
Toe bones

Desiring fish
Would empty
Our buoyancy
Aim us
Through our
Surface image

Life Drawing: After Nightmare

just a dream,
honey, only a
dream. draw yourself
through the room
of heartbeat. make
five minutes to
hang on with
the light scurry
of the pencil
the brush sound
of the hand
adjusting like wind
to snow, sand
to ocean, as
the hand draws
the line across
and returns to
show you where
you are in
relation to the
others, the model
who breathes, the
paper, the line
you make of it.

Pay Attention Here Until

The starting line
The line of the body
The line between
Before, after
Timeline
Bioline
The line that repeats
Circumference
The resumed line
The waiting line
The line that disappears
Of adjacency
Of ascension
The recline
Story line
Maternal
Paternal
XY
Out of line
The fault line
The selvedge
The line that indicates
Sightline
Trajectory
The boundary line
The line that elides
Fish life rush trip
Of traffic
Of argument
Of code
Of song
The horizon line
The line that elides

In on off out
Crossing the
Walking the
Holding the
Letting out the
The end of the line

Pay Attention Here Until

At last, I no longer know how to draw

—Matisse

What defines us as humans is certainly not language, not tool making, not memory, not the unwillingness to die, not regret, not, god knows, empathy. Maybe we don't know because we cannot agree on a definition of "we"—I can't agree on a definition of we. Maybe it is, simply and disastrously, that we draw lines, that we—I—love the linear too much. The straight shot.

And yet, in our tibias, said to be our straightest bones, cells spiral.

For premise, let "we" be our common neurobiology, a shared score for body-mind within which individuals move as they move. Why do we draw lines when lines do not exist? Our world is not first inked with outlines, then filled in, or out. And yet.

We draw lines because lines are a language that even babies understand, because the lines we draw are contours and contours are nongradual changes in our visual field, because we are designed to pay attention to what is discontinuous, because we live and move in space and time and because we are predator and prey.

I am prey and predator. So are animals, fish, and trees, but somewhere along the line, the main line became a power line. The straight shot. The flatline.

Once I was in a dance workshop for improving alignment. The teacher was working with a composed, confident woman as we observed. He had many questions for her. "Why did you move your shoulder like that?" "What were you thinking when you did this?" and "Why did you think that?" The woman disintegrated while he pushed and prodded. I wish I could forget how her voice pitched. "Are you telling me," she said, "That my problem is I was raped? That everything, everything, always goes back to that? I am always and forever raped?"

Prey and prey on. I tried listing all those I have injured, exploited, consumed. There are so many ways to harm. My handwriting cramped. I fell mute, then immobile. And yet, I continue.

The straight shot. The flatline.

I draw a lot of lines. The reason is I am prey. The reason is I am predator + Two lines mark the spot I must pay attention to until I no longer know how to draw.

A Question of Karma

Nightmare's Aubade

Long I have been
your nightly lover
ravishing you. Mine.
Pinned you to our
bed, my hand on your
mouth, my other prowling
your private, your
impossible
mythologies in
illogical blood
red rooms. How I
loved misshaping
the mansion of you.
How I have loved.
My obsidian
cloak falls from you now
too familiarly.
All the night jewels slip
from your hair, from
your fingers. In
remembrance, I pluck
your last lapis.

This is a silent poem, it will not flow

—Laura Jensen

Rothko said *silence is so accurate*.
Yes and no. Silence is a color, is
A pace.
Now frozen. The news.
                                        The news.
The space heater shushes the dog paddling
Out of dreams, the old furnace
Knocks nine knocks.
The good china is latched with
                                        A latch.

Eve

Alpha may merely mean first,
As in Eve.
Eve is the skin
Of an old day.
Do not shame her
For her hunger
From raising you,
Nightfall.

Alpha may merely mean parent,
As in parenthesis
(from the Latin
As in Eve. How easy
To disregard that which
Supports. There is always
Another, even
If missing.

Alpha may merely mean pathmaker
In deep snow
In strong wind
For others to walk, fly
More easily.
When alpha tires,
The letters rearrange.
No big deal

Except, some do not
Follow. Looking at you,
Adam.

No. 2, Mark Rothko, 1963: Portrait of a Nice Stranger

She thought maybe this business about *meaning* was only to be someone people could tell things to. Maybe she was only supposed to listen, only carry what people told her for as long as she remembered. Because people, usually people who did not know her at all, or well, told her things, things they usually would not say or would never say to anyone else. Painful things. She did not know why people did this. It was mildly surprising. Because she was invisible. Maybe that was why. Her heart felt scoured most of the time. Was this heart trouble or just heart? The thing about doctors, if you asked them, they would find some trouble, and did she want to know? Not really, no. Sometimes her heart banged her awake at night and sometimes it walked along the marsh, where it looks like good ground, but it gives. The color of lying awake at night is dried blood. That bar of sunset? That's salmon hope. Why did she think that? When she no longer remembered what someone told her, there remained the dust of what they said. The motes lay themselves down in her in lanes, loss like air in lungs filling from the bottom. Did you know? Dust grows quite heavy. The salmon row the space that's left.

A Question of Karma

Whatever it was,
it burst when
the acupuncturist slipped
a needle into
something held taut
as a balloon
blown up past
safety, popped. Whatever
it was rushed
out of my
eyes, out of
my muscles, quaked
my body. The
acupuncturist, like a
seamstress working on
a garment turned
wrong side out,
calmly continued
inserting her pins.

Ides of March

1.

We found it harder and harder to stay close
To one another. No one had time
To nurture friendships. We worked so hard
All the time then, and there was no time.
At the end of the world were two tired
Untouched people trying to finish
The work they misunderstood was theirs.

2.

The mosquito that did not die that winter
Is moaning with the train, the kind of
Crying one cries when the crying won't
Run down, when lungs are torn concertinas.
There's never a last mosquito,
Never a last train. There's more
Yeah, there's more, endless, sorrow.
We don't know where it all keeps
Coming from, or care, want
The miseries to stop, stop, for sleep.

The Ability to Wait

Night now, and day, the lone baby bird lies in a dollar store basket I tied to the awning after watching its too-thin mother return again and again to the bracings with a mate who clearly was not invested. Every year the red-dusted house finches come and stuff some slight twigs into the hollow metal support tube raked at a precarious angle and every year they abandon the site, too long, too narrow, too nearly vertical. The too-thin finch left too. Then the city cut down hundreds of allegedly diseased, lush trees; it rained, deluged a month; and the even-thinner finch returned alone, just standing here outside the brace with a twig from the bridal wreath, one pert leaf at half-mast. She seemed frankly overwhelmed. I have been working and sleeping at the awninged window, so I know a little about one-room living. The dollar store is surprisingly abundant. I found a small woven basket in Floral and yellow twine in Automotive. I didn't think it worked; the finch was nowhere to be seen. But one morning, a gaunt head arose from the basket and gazed at me. The great thing about baby birds is they do that, they look right at you as if you are benign or even bird. The thin finch has returned only twice to feed the too-quiet baby in these many days. The baby never cheeps. This finch was born to sing the rose world open but even birds need a mentor and a second genre. The ability to wait, silent and motionless, for someone who is not coming does not count.

Her Daughter Will Find Her Diary and It Will Be Blank, Except the First Page, One Sentence

Fritz went into town today.
The impulse to—
even Blessed Mary is distant

Fritz went into town today.
My day
but I am not in it

Fritz went into town today.
And tomorrow Fritz will be here
that is as usual so I will not write that down

Fritz went into town today.
The air is so heavy
All the letters begin
"I'm sorry I haven't written"

Fritz went into town today.
I am not altogether sure
that no one will read this. With three
children under eight, only wind
to talk to and it takes my words
right from me. The children are
watchers
I can't cry out, can't escape leave
even to the hilltop or woods
the oldest, it's too much for her,
she feels my need

Fritz went into town today.
It's difficult to be someone different
than everyone knows you to be

Fritz went into town today.
This diary
its unmasking pages

Fritz went into town today.
Why do these words stop me?
So many words form history
but they are Czech words, old words

Fritz went into town today.
The wind never stops
I can't explain why this makes me
Fritz says I should not be so anxious

Fritz went into town today.

Falling Water Blues

Fall is an old word, older than water
A waterfall is water's second falling
Fall is an old word, the falling of water
The surprise we have visceral memory of

A lush slip in a slash, a dash, a flush
Lapis, sapphire, topaz, and turquoise
Lush slip in a slash, a diamond flush
A dishevel releasing the blues

One of those blues is the blue of Kae's eyes
Blue flag, hydrangea, phlox, and larkspur
Flashed heron, flashed sky in the blue of Kae's eyes
And the creek hummed in her blue-black hair

The real show is the pool below, the vie, the vault, the breach
Froths of baby's breath and Queen Anne's lace, calla and daisy
The pool below, the vie, the vault, the breach, and smackdown
Sports and spouts, loosed, effusive, lily of the valley

Now see Kae in the aster shadow there
See she gave by volition and violation
Her blues bruised, Kae is the echinacea there
Blazing star falling, out of the bluing sun

Fall is an old word, older than water
A waterfall is water's second falling
Fall is an old word, the falling of water
The surprise we have visceral memory of

I Meant to Write Love

I Give You Long Low Clouds

To cool your forehead and dampen your noisy thoughts.

I give you low rumbling thunder to sing to your
Heart in her native tongue so she may be consoled.

I give you a field stone to fit in the den of your thumb and first finger.
It colors when wet. Spit. Cry.

There are trees in your heart to hold your nests.
Deep roots release you into motion and support you in rest.

O the windows rattle in adoration.
The house is moved to open her stairs and speak.

I give you long low clouds

Short Night

After Buson

Solstice taps the weight
Dusk, small bathing sounds of carp
Orioles jump reeds

Night sky colander
Remember playing aliens?
Flash drives, cell phones, souls

Short night —
Clematis rest from giving
Mouth full, rabbit speaks

Floating in the Ocean, Rincon, Puerto Rico

The ocean gave me baby legs, folding
And unfolding like paper accordions.
Jostled like a troublesome baby, I grasped
My swimming noodle with a baby's reflex
Grip because you can trust the ocean
Not to care too much about your breath,
Your body. It's all one thing, a cradle.
Mother's breath blowing across boo boos.
At night, she pulls back darkness
From the shore, lifts it, beats it, throws it
Down with a boom. Boom, boom.

Dance Class

I would break
Into blossom

—James Wright

The wings of the newly emerged butterfly are small
She needs to pump them up with fluid from her abdomen.
Each Saturday we come for dance class
Breath by breath, dropping, deepening
Into movement, our first body.
Overcurves, undercurves, dangles, bends, tossing, catching
We know how to do this.
We coax ourselves with breath, momentum, pattern.
We align ourselves with ourselves, radiating, radiant, resonant

What It Was Like Today, Saturday, October 17

The dog circled herself so fast just because
Because because.
A girl twirling in her skirt makes her own
Spinning earth.
Nine adults worked to master a phrase of dance,
With attack and
Lyricism. Play play. We are our bodies,
We are not our
Bodies, we light candles for bodies.
Just for the game
Of getting it back, the dog buries her ball.
What it was like today was to keep moving.

Cells

The cells of your hands bow my cells
I am wood taking shape in your hands
I am a cello in your hands

Nabi Conversation Tear

Don't be afraid of painting it

—Gauguin, October, 1888

Here?
It's too much
and not
enough to
check
the ex-
honest,
the ve-
nomous,
the merely
used,
from the
privi-
lege of req
uisite
self-service.
I stay, but
warily,
hours
too easily
mesh,
drain,
I couldn't— "
But
" said
Ahmad,
like Gauguin
to Sérusier,

I could (or
should? ould?)
—our connection
dismal,
synthetic—
have
asked my
e freedom
to re-mark
that blueness "
as blue as
wren (or
children? ren?)
" Our
connection
dismal,
synthetic
or lost. I
settled
the phone
in Nabi
landscape, the
most green
on my
palette.

Still Life: After a Suicide on Campus

For no reason, a student
brought me a cup of hot tea.
"Do you like Earl Grey?"
And—was it only this morning?—
the cashier handed me
a small bag, separate from my groceries.
"I figured this was your lunch,"
she said, "I hope that's okay."

p.s., a friend texted, *I meant to write love not live*
but it read live not live
        (liv not liv)
Why is there no love today in the auto-lexicon?
And yet
        the cashier
        the student
        the student who—
The students from the college across the river put a flower
in every campus PO box here, walls of flowers.

The family wants privacy, but death is public.
We have held some of us back from that death.
Some of us have held ourselves back.
Everyone knows someone who—

I walk across campus with my hot tea,
think of the cashier putting my deli chicken,
honey mustard, napkin, and Coke
in a separate, small bag. No.
Death is private. And death's privacy asks us

to not protect our gentleness
too much. I look in my friend's
office window and see her street shoes,
shaped like her feet.
They tell me not to wait,
She's out dancing.

This is not a platitude; it's her job.
She teaches dance, composition of the bodymind.
Her empty shoes join the tea, the lunch bag,
and the flowers in this day's still life.

Give, We Say

Fields having given look used.
Are we satisfied with wrest?
When mother said *there is no*
Meaning, did she say *sometimes?*
It makes a difference, and a field
At night, does it lie awake?

When the sky is loneliest
Without clouds, without moon,
Without heron or goose,
The stars give, we say, light.

Prayer and Real Prayer

Dog and I look out the window together
every morning. It's how we pray. Dog sniffs
two in-breaths for each of mine. One of hers
is for breath and one's for deconstructing air.
I cannot follow her findings. I can
follow trees. What I like about trees is,
even though they are incredibly busy,
they're peaceable. Which reminds me, at least
one person somewhere, this very second
prays real prayers for all beings. *May we be*
free from suffering. May we be calm, very
calm. May no one set off a nuclear
bomb. That someone prays at any given
moment is one reassuring aspect
of there being far too many people
on the planet. Another is, I think
my chances for love have increased with age,
rather than declined as statistics say,
provided no one blows up the planet.
The planet seems to be doing her best
to blow us up, but collectively we
resist her interventions. *May we be*
free from suffering. Keep praying, dear you
thinking now to get coffee, to get to work,
keep praying a few more seconds, while dog
sighs, and I pick up my pen to thank you.

We Come In from the Stars

It had been a quiet day
We had been too moved by the sky
To speak, by the lake
Too moved, a loon
Plays against its echo

Perfect, such that more stars
Peer through space
Unfolding as if stored space
Kept like pleated paper lanterns
They have died, the stars

"Too late" seems to be our sky
And yet, from this folded day
May I pull from the lake
Love into depth, more than echo
May I wed beneath paper lanterns

In the Sunshine Hey

Between we two friends, she is the optimist
But only I can believe the sun will return
And it does.

In the sunshine, she plays rounds of solitaire.
Each time she declares, "I better win this one."
Hers is a willed

Optimism. Mine is observed. In the sunshine
I read Laura Jensen, her assertive birds. Had she
Ever wholly rested?

Have I? Maybe I will never again
Write. I want images. No more words. Laura
Lost me. Maybe

I can use this formula of Laura's line.
Hey (a jay) Hey Hey (wheezing like a sorry
Dog toy. One answers, barks like a dog maybe
A sorry dog)

In the sunshine Hey in the sunshine my friend
Puts things to order, 5, 4, 3 Hey Hey in
The sunshine gleams the optimist's spade, brightens
The observed heart

To Get Outside of Ourselves

Some of us align with trees, with their familiar
largos. Each tree's a world of water, but do not

mistake that world for tree. Same goes for us. The god
of water is the moon, which is, as far as we

know, an agent of gravity that masquerades
as light, so we reached for the moon. It is said, when

we evolved to standing—you believe we evolved?—
we lost function in our tails. Tails, according to

dogs, are for expressing joy, curiosity,
fear, and for wrapping oneself up. Also jumping!

For these, trees don't have tails but do have branches. Just
now, a buck pulled that pine branch like a bell rope. Then

what do you suppose when he looked in my window?
For a moment, we made a ring of attention,

like mirrors placed on opposing walls, looking at
themselves. We felt mirror-distant, distance being

a function of light. For example, did you read
the program notes? I always do; I want to know

just what the creator was thinking. "Why," it said,
"rely on the structure of two opposing things?"

We *rely* because we must, just as a tree can't
not grow. Reliance is a function of being

human. As for the *structure of twos*, don't you think
this is passé? "On a spectrum" seems au courant,

but that, also, is too linear. How about:
let us rely on the structure of ringing things:

Odes

Ode to Anon

O the light, as others give it to us;
Water, sand, birds, flash it to us.
I still remember, years ago, on the bus,
My held-back impulse to lean forward,
Gently say, "Sir, there are rainbows in your hair."
The set of the man's shoulders
Suggested he did not know this way in which
He was beautiful, that the sun
Chose him, of all the people on the right-hand side
Of the bus, rows 1 through 15,
To alight, to adorn. I withheld. Perhaps
It was spring, gritty and drab.
Certainly, I was weary. Anonymous
You, did anyone ever tell you?

Ode to Art

This black bird with sunset sleeves
Scolds, backsucking two *n*'s
Is everyone who wished you away

Brush it into a painting with text
Fluttering down, little shelters

Ode to the Graveyard

Remember the gravel
Along the road, however
Lowly, some glitter with
Copper, some with silver, some
Ask to be scuffed to surface

Ode to Minneapolis in Winter, in Answer to the Woman from Georgia, Here for the Super Bowl, Who, When Interviewed on TV, Kept Asking "How Do You Live Here?"

The first snow, which fell a month
Ago, was perfect, and tricked
Us into remembering what we would
Like to believe always but is almost
Never true, in the city anyway,
Which is what the second snow was, the true
Snow which comes as rain and turns to ugly
Ice. Today, all of us driving to work
Was like mass tobogganing with lethal
Motors and I know I was not the only
One running through the list that's like
A mantra: I live here because my friends
Are here, my family's here, my work is here.
I live here because what would I do without
My writing group every Monday, my dance
Class every Saturday. I live here
Because I can't think where else I could live
Or how I could pull it off. I'm so cold.
Maybe someday. But my friends are here,
My family is here, my work is here.
For symbols, chattering teeth.
For bass drum, car wheels over ice ruts.
When the expats text and post weather
Reports of 60 degrees and sun,
The part of me that never gets warm says
It's no fun anymore, you can't ski, can't

Even walk, it's so slippery. My friends
Are here, family is here, work is here.
And it's so dark. Friends here, family here.
And that's really all there is to say
About it. You can move! the expats write,
Giddy with escape. I can, sure
But then I don't.

Ode to the Migraine

Observe
The ode
You
Earned
Passing
Here
Likea
Para
De thro
Ugh
A
Pinh
Ole

Ode to Instinct

Instinct, if you have it,
is a kind of gravity.
My dog's whole being
knows that
not visible to me—
it vibrates
through the leash.
Sometimes we run
after rabbits within
her knowing, my
not-knowing, too fast
to watch the ground
to place my feet—
they place themselves.

Ode to the Lonsdale Area Phone Book

I have always loved
the encyclopedic
headings of
phone books;
the companionship
of advertising
– air, cellular – chambers,
electric – erosion,
exercise – feed,
government – guns,
gutters – hearing,
laser – liquors,
printers – railroads,
real – religious,
surveyors – tanning,
taverns – taxidermists

Poetry made
by the industry
of words and people,
objects and services,
catalogs of life.
All that wisdom
practicality and serendipity
– serenity

The Saint Paul
yellow pages
are as thick
as the Compact
Edition OED, A–O.

The Lonsdale phone
book is about
as thick as an average
"New and Selected"
collection of poems.

In Japan, according
to Kwong-Roshi,
when you move,
it is customary
to cook a certain
hot dish for your neighbors
—the name of the noodle
translates loosely to
"I moved near you."

Something about finding,
or being found,
or filing.
A place
for everything
should mean a place
for everyone.
Rough, yellow
Tissue beatifies
– beautifies

Ode to the To Do List

• You call me, wake me
– You give purpose to my day
– Or semblance of purpose
• You give direction, your lean is cleaner than lust
• You defy aging. You're self-renewing, perennial
– Why, you look as young as the day you were born, lovely long enumerations
– Any amputations and you grow limbs
• Cheerleader, you remind me what I have accomplished
– Encourage
– Cajole
– "First in ten, do it again!"
– *Listy (adj.) pleasant, willing (to do something)*
• Your love is tougher than a wish list
– Less drama than a bucket list
– More treble than a playlist
• You're more democratic than an A list
– *Spenser, if no one else, tried listful*
• You're as loyal as a backlist
– A dog under my heels at every turn
– A stable horse who knows the trail too well
• *And to his doome with listfull ears did both attend*

Ode to the Toaster

I don't know what would happen if I put my bread
In the couple's slot of the toaster.

I dutifully put my single slice
In the single's slot. But

The couple's slot looks brighter,
Feels hotter, and I want, O—

I want my slice to go down and rise up charged,
Heat-sweetened with another.

Ode to My Frozen Shoulder

What armistice is this?
Shoulder, you're a killdeer
dragging wing to distract
from the nest, but what's in
the nest? Is that your point?
You are a post-modern
shoulder, deconstructing,
making an arm of function
into form. You've taken
a stand, so to speak,
against dichotomy,
the binary, left versus
right, you've claimed my arm on
a spectrum of rightness.
You have obliged a
consolation ribbon,
a peace pole. An easily
kept pet, leashed to me like
a service animal,
quiet, present. You're a
butterfly, self-casted,
in metamorphosis,
an optimist, an ahead-
of-schedule angel wing.
You're a holding tank for
my exhaustion. A glass
ceiling. My daydream, ten
percent of me on stay-
cation. A backbending
dance, the limbo of push
and pull. A breach of reach.
A lame duck, a pacifist
ant. A shy kid at the door
of the party. A bell

rope, a knotted chain. A
jointy deer. A Tin Man
caught without his Dorothy.
A cat stuck in a tree,
left out, ladderless. Left
leaning. A pen without
ink, anything you write
is above reproach. A
megaphone for stillness.
Out on a limb, you're trans-
limb, redefining limbness,
liminal. You are the
gestalt of arm, armature.
You're open, full, pitted,
a chair, a force, a hole,
a band, an edge, a twist.
The Limpopo river.
A limpet, adhered to
tidal me. A numb blade.
A loaf, a llama, a lamb.
On the lam, lawless. An
armadillo, burrowed
into itself, balled. You're
Armageddon to reckon,
finally, my evil with
my good. You're the chauffeur
fourteen paces past the
limousine, nursing a
cigarette in bitter
wind. You portend death, lest
I forget the end of
the world hangs on me.
I don't say it enough,
shoulder, I love you.

Ode to Odes

Not Grecian urns nor nightingales
Not west wind nor Aeolus's harp
Not melancholy nor solitude
Not immortality nor shoes
Not duty nor Aphrodite
Not drum nor Confederate dead
Not joy, nor Spot, nor Billy Joe
It's odes themselves I'm grateful for

Laughing, clapping, wave-you-in odes
Awesome, reverent stand-back odes
Love-drunk, moony, proposing odes
Fancy, playful, imagine-that odes
Iambic, rhyming, schematic odes
Freewheeling, hop-on-the-bus odes
Busting-out academics' odes
Whistling, wouldya looky-this odes

O Odes!
That something works for someone somewhere
Right now, works for me!

Notes

The process of writing "The Memoir of Mona Lisa" was, first, acts of looking, seeing, and watching; second, acts of historical and art research; and third, acts of imaginative inhabiting of Mona Lisa, the painting and the woman. These immersive acts supported my guesses and leaps.

Thanks to Erin Thompson for the phrase "mail my hand" in "Letter from Spain."

"Some of Us Are Drawn to Those Who Don't Want Us" is dedicated to Andrea Matthews Clark and the Wildlife Rehabilitation Center of Minnesota.

For "Pay Attention Here Until" I thank Margaret Livingstone, author of *Vision and Art: The Biology of Seeing*, for helping me figure out why we draw lines, when in fact, lines in nature rarely exist.

"A Question of Karma" is dedicated to Jennifer Connell.

"Falling Water Blues" is for Kae Frances and is after the painting "Falling Water #6 (Traces of Minnehaha Falls)" by Marcia Söderman.

Thanks to Deborah Keenan for the title "What It Was Like Today."

"Nabi Conversation Tear" is inspired by the torn edge of a found poem by Deborah Keenan.

"In the Sunshine Icy" is dedicated to Becky Heist.

"To Get Outside of Ourselves" is dedicated to Judith Howard. It quotes, out of context, her program notes for *Central Supply*.

"Ode to the To Do List" quotes *Online Etymology Dictionary* and *Faerie Queene* (25.9).

Acknowledgments

I am grateful to the editorial and production teams of the publications in which the following poems first appeared, sometimes in earlier versions: *Nimrod International Journal, Poetry City, Unamuno Author Series #22*, and *Short Night*.

"Her Daughter Will Find Her Diary and It Will Be Blank, Except the First Page, One Sentence" was performed as libretto for choreography, commissioned and performed by Brianna Hall, with premieres in 2009 in Northfield and Minneapolis, Minnesota.

Curators Lee Kisling, Lana Sjoberg, and Margaret Welshons commissioned the poem "Falling Water Blues" as a response piece to the painting "Falling Water #6 (Traces of Minnehaha Falls)" by Marcia Söderman, for the exhibition *Sister Arts: Poetry and Visual Art* at The Phipps Center for the Arts, Hudson, Wisconsin. They also selected "We Come In from the Stars" as a subject piece for the exhibit.

I thank all the readers of the many drafts of "The Memoir of Mona Lisa," including Liz Engelman, Patricia Weaver Francisco, Deborah Keenan, Teresa Klotz, Jim Moore, Alison Morse, Yvette Nelson, Sheila O'Connor, Charles Preble, and Suzanne Swanson who were especially generous with questions and comments. Joanne Smallen assisted with research. Jane Peck provided a gift of time to research and write at her cabin in Lanesboro, Minnesota. A residency fellowship from Tofte Lake Center, with funds from the Jerome Foundation, provided time to revise "The Memoir of Mona Lisa."

I am grateful to Spencer Reece, Desperate Literature, and American Space Madrid for inviting me to Madrid for the Unamuno Author Series and a weeklong residency during which I wrote the poems in the "Letter from Spain" section.

Many of the poems in "Lines That Do Not Exist but We Draw Them" were written with fellowship support from the Vermont Studio Center.

For poems in "I Meant to Write Love," I thank Becky Heist, Tom O'Connell, Stephanie Lindeman, and Dean Lindeman for time spent writing at their family cabin on Lake Vermillion, and I thank Judith Anderson for time spent writing at her home in Rincon, Puerto Rico.

For ongoing inspiration and nurturance, I thank my J team, the Klatch, Monday Poets, Raelani Greenlee, Holly Harden, Athena Kildegaard, Tilly Strauss, Maya Washington, and Tammy Darrah Wenberg. Thanks also to Coco, good dog and office manager.

I especially thank my publisher, Jessie Lendennie, for her faith in this book, and Siobhán Hutson for making it beautiful.

Finally, I thank you, dear Reader.

SU LOVE is the author of six collections of poetry; she previously published as Su Smallen. Her work has been recognized with, notably, the Jane Kenyon Poetry Prize and residencies with the St. Croix Watershed Research Station and Tofte Lake Center in Minnesota and the Unamuno Author Series in Madrid. Su is a 2019 recipient of an Artist Initiative grant from the Minnesota State Arts Board.

salmonpoetry

Cliffs of Moher, County Clare, Ireland

"Like the sea-run Steelhead salmon that thrashes upstream to its spawning ground, then instead of dying, returns to the sea – Salmon Poetry Press brings precious cargo to both Ireland and America in the poetry it publishes, then carries that select work to its readership against incalculable odds."

TESS GALLAGHER

The Salmon Bookshop & Literary Centre

Ennistymon, County Clare, Ireland

Listed in *The Irish Times'* 35 Best Independent Bookshops